Breaking

Breaking

poems by
Buffy Aakaash

SHANTI ARTS PUBLISHING
BRUNSWICK, MAINE

Breaking

Published by Shanti Arts LLC
193 Hillside Road
Brunswick, Maine 04011

shantiarts.com

Designed by Shanti Arts Designs

Cover images— paris-bilal / RxhytSvxKGw / unsplash.com; mohith-sarma / tCgWLm6VR7U / unsplash.com (background image)

Printed in the United States of America

ISBN: 978-1-956056-93-8 (softcover)

Library of Congress Control Number (LCCN): 2025949411

To All My Loves…
You know who you are.

Contents

THE BEAUTY BEFORE US

Acknowledgments

The author is grateful to the editors of the following publications in which these poems first appeared:

Avocet: "Desire" (Spring 2007)

Dissonance Magazine: "Read the Warnings and Guidelines Before Proceeding" (as "What Love is Never"; Spring 2021)

Into the Glen—Into the Light: "The Goat Boutique" (Summer 2021)

Iris Literary Journal: "Amore" (2020)

Love Anthology (published by Bronze Bird Books, Summer 2024): "A Late Epiphany" (as "Commitment")

MONO X online erotica: "Nothing and Everything" (December 2021)

The Mountain Troubadour (anthology, published by the Poetry Society of Vermont): "The Beauty Before Us" (received the Marian Gleason Memorial Award)

The North: "Remembering Last Year at Hood Canal" (Summer 2022)

Planisphere Q: "The Things I Can Now See Without You"(Spring 2022)

The Poet Magazine (UK): "Conception" (as "About My Birth"; Winter 2021)

The Raven's Perch: "Anchoring" (Spring 2021)

The Soliloquist: "Spring Equinox" (Spring 2025)

The Whiskey Blog: "Cowboy Regrets"(Spring 2022)

The Write Launch: "Fly Balls"; "Infinite Affair With Air"; and "Love Letters" (Spring 2020)

Untangling the Knots (chapbook, published by Kelsay Books, 2022): "How to Die" and "How to Start Over"

Wild Word: "One Tennessee Summer" (Spring 2024)

From the poet:

I extend my great appreciation to the many who helped me put this book together:

... to the 25-plus-year-old Otter Creek Poets in Middlebury, Vermont. My reading of these poems there prompted many edits and revisions;

... to my masterful poet friends who reviewed early, then later versions of this book: creative extraordinaire Maxima Kahn and fellow Vermont poet Cindy Ellen Hill;

... to Julene Tripp Weaver and Ray Hudson for excellent revision suggestions. Thanks to the people and programs who helped me think in new ways: the wonderful staff and faculty at Vermont College of Fine Arts, Joan Houlihan at the Colrain Poetry Manuscript Conference, and to the fine tutelage of master-poet Eduardo Corral.

I want to thank all the journals, individuals, and small publishers who print and share poems from "unknown" poets of promise. Specifically, Christine Cote of Shanti Arts LLC, for publishing this book, and Kelsay Books for publishing my chapbook, *Untangling the Knots*.

I must also give hearty thanks to the Vermont Arts Council and the Vermont Community Foundation, supported by the National Endowment for the Arts, for supporting me with an artist development grant.

And of course to "all my loves" for the experiences that inspired me to write every single one of these poems.

Buffy Aakaash
East Calais, Vermont
September 22, 2025

"A fractal is a never-ending pattern. Fractals are infinitely complex patterns that are self-similar across different scales. They are created by repeating a simple process over and over in an ongoing feedback loop. Driven by recursion, fractals are images of dynamic systems—the pictures of Chaos. Geometrically, they exist in between our familiar dimensions. Fractal patterns are extremely familiar, since nature is full of fractals."

—from FractalFoundation.org

CONCEPTION

Fly Balls

I was never very good at sensing the trajectory of high fliers
and in fact once caught a fly ball with my eye socket
ending my dalliance with baseball.

How quickly I healed, but today
bones are liable to shatter.
Bruises from brazen encounters linger. I still

fear that flying hard ball, myself out in left field, looking up,
balancing an awkwardly oversized mitt, with the bright sun
of a good life blinding me from what's to come.

Conception

Born in September,
I was but a "twinkle" in December,
trees without a single leaf, all
fallen,
frozen,
crunching underneath
my parents' young and nimble feet.

Yes,
the day   I   s p r u n g
from "just   a   thought"
the   skies   were   overcast
and   Jersey   lakes   I've   come   to   know
were   gray   and   frozen,

my   parents   having   chosen
some   side   trip   through   color
through   cracks   in   cold   veneer
safely   beyond   the   fear   and   swelter,
slightly   dappling   leaves,

then   here   I   was   d e l i v e r e d
on   an   autumn   breeze

falling
with
them
again.

The Goat Boutique

If you go in
you might come out.
You might come out
looking better than before
you went in:
tussled with musty rose lips
a dusting of glitter
the visage of a horned god within you
revealed behind vertical pupils.
You may find a little shift here
you've never seen anywhere else.
Mystified you wonder if humans
are not the only visitors,
if some other
might come home
with you, wanted or otherwise.

If you go in
you will be changed
either within or without
or in your whole being.
Perhaps what you come out wearing
merits tearing in careful rips,
your naked self unveiled, receptive, inquisitive.
These chance "ribbons" wrapped
with rotational intention
around a protuberant maypole.
Maybe next year
you will show restraint
at the door and then—
go in anyway,
the festive boutique
and the magic goat

in your soul.

Anchoring

Through our eyes
this warm lap of timelessness,
where I have not been
since my first day here,
when you took me in,
beheld me, and drank me,

will anchor me

now that you go
taking with you
that undying love
that limitless compassion
strength only a mother can muster
bringing forth her child.

No Shame in Love

I tell my friend: *Every child*
deserves to know where he came from.
You question your paternity,
the vague accounts of your origin
from your father, the most righteous
one who left you in your mother.
And you fear the festering wounds
as you look behind the shadows.

Hereditary facts affirm
truths for others soon forgotten.
Tales of minor misdeeds reveal
the exploits his parents questioned.
I tell him there's no shame in love
that engendered his conception.

Maternal Sympathies

Chair,
wheelchair,
cold linoleum floor,
self and other.
Oxygen,
flowery spreads,
inhaling and exhaling
self and other.

She wonders if I'm here,
and, if so, just barely.
Will I be here for dinner?
(As if we'll seem more, then.)
And, if not, when
will I next come?
She acknowledges me,
but not with enough
      self presence
            to be sure of anything.

My wellness is more to the point.
I need tea and chocolate
more than she does conversation.
That's what she said,
more or less.
I would like
for one moment
to be one
without the other.
            And we are.

When we see each other and smile.
And she sings to me about enchanted evenings.
And everything goes fluffy around us.
And I hold her hand ...
And rub her dry skin
with simple exfoliating joys,
removing a cat's tongue of fear
                    from her world.

Eliot Is Dead

—dedicated to my teacher Eliot Cowan,
Huichol healer, and author of *Plant Spirit Medicine*

About a year it's been my teacher is dead.
Tradition requires time to honor the dead.

Today they gather on the land he sanctified
opening gates to mourners who forward the dead.

We trust divine teaching (until it is rote),
words of godly relations who father the dead.

With the beloved I did not always agree
but in truth it's best we do not bother the dead.

The master's mind and heart battled each other,
as they do he said in all of us until we coffer the dead.

Following my heart he perceived I'd been deceived,
conjuring his faithful logic in order to ponder the dead.

O master this portion of life I do not know.
Share with me your wisdom now you are dead.

This elder said to honor my name from birth.
So I am Peter Buffy now and then until I am dead.

The Recording

She speaks without words.
I ask what she's saying
and she says
Nothing. Essentially true.
I wonder what she sees
through me, around me,
this vision,
only pure emotion,
not spoken,
rewound and replayed.

My touch
or a hearty laugh
opens her eyes,
reminds her of the body –
of phrases
of light
of myself and herself,
but still
(Damn this cognition!)
the recording is blank.

Coitus Interruptus

We rang in the annual
chime in time
so we'd not forget
the months between
our singing
of Old Lang Syne.
Our lines and curves
tumbled and rolled,
electric lips
and tangled tongues
our eyes that meet
halfway to Heaven.
In that late hour of love
came puzzles and heavy blows.
Bodies locked in New Year bliss
a bondage scene
without any grace.

It was Mother dying
that forced a funeral
for time and space.
Mothers always die,
a never-ending end
even after the television
goes off.

When Mother dies:
stillness tortures us
as we conduct
a postmortem
of ecstatic moments
we saw expired in our wake.

How to Die

My father left behind so many miracles:

sun dappling the wall in the afternoon
breeze through an open window

We held hands, hearts in sync, ancestral kinship
through his mother's eyes and straight through mine

Often first across the finish line this humble
gamesmanship his only diversion

from a life graciously arranged through time
a plotting of loving deeds done in earnest.

His Quaker roots planted deep this divine
equanimity gently guiding rarely demanding

His branches burst with his flowering treasures:
the good children he knew we were and would be.

In our final moments: he worried I would die young
in that last great pandemic he watched claim my brother

With a glance through the window he took in that sun.
Wind rustled the trees, and at last he knew he could

let me go.

    And I him.

Infinite Affair with Air

You are this
which is not
that,
that
which is not
this.
You owe such and such
to whoever and whom,
need all of that
to accomplish this,
and could never be those
because you are these.

But maybe this once,
you make some amends,
excepting this, that, and the other thing,
as well as such and such.
"How long will *this* last?"
someone asks.
You are all these things,
you reply,
but not all those,
and tomorrow, all of those,
but not all of these.
(How dare they question!)

All I want to know is
Who am I in all of this?
Who will I be in all of that?
Are you anywhere always?
Or always somewhere at least?
Because I am here now and
tomorrow I may be there.

Sitting with Mother

I come and go
in the span of a moment
so fast in her eyes.

Infinitely long
it seems I am gone
too quick I am here.

In just that moment
we pick out tulips for spring
to brighten the cold.

A Late Epiphany

In commitment
you hold in high regard
something beyond your limited self.

Something you know raises up the world.
The existence of Love itself:
You muster it for all it is worth.

Its unfolding from your gut.
Shining from your chest.
Exploding from your crown.

No Telling

There's no telling,
Love. It has no end. No beginning.
Always in the middle
of so many stories.
Each one ending in death,

yet still they go on.

Grandmother tells them.
Love, she says,
*there's just no telling
what will become.*

LOVE IS A FRACTAL

The Catch

As these men fish me
for some kind of love,
I too drop a line
into those depths,

only to catch a tale
of deep sorrows,
the great white
of my delusions.

At the end of this
otherwise perfect day,
I wash up as food
for scavengers,

stinking in the sun,
nothing ahead of me
but lies in a bottle,
corpses of untruth strewn

across my beach
of gritty stories,
my line of feelers
out in the waves, thinking

when they take this bait,
my love will come home.

There's the catch.

Desire

Within me grow trees
seeded in other times
scarce of heartwood,
a sapling perhaps
nurtured many years,
pruned for eternal youth:

a bonsai of my perfect
desire for luscious
leaves, prolific limbs,
shallow revered
roots strangling
with juvenile strife.

Today I split its wood
to feed a fire
in the aging forest
of my history
as if this sacrifice
will suffice.

As if,

as if somewhere this lavish stand,
this bountiful wood ushered
through a gateway of burning,
will give honorable passage
to the naive longings
I will shed.

Amore

Drunk on heavenly amber,
that ancient yellow gem
of the earth wafting
from his neck, dancing
for a moment away
from the world of
linear progressions.
I could not turn away
and brushed his sweet
lips with my own
into a union with
the whirling scent
of shining sun.
Rays of mutual desire
shaded by my wall
of personal
refrain I falter
in pleasant
stupor.

Bittersweet

Everything acrid now
in my foaming
rabid mouth

goes sublime this time
with that gem
of a lost snippet

when he stripped down
with me at the pond
and we slipped up

the muddy bank
later wrapped in sullied
sheets away shaded

from New Mexico sun.
Now my mascot's
portrayal of this queer love

activates my lingering
tastes on film
all the way from Cannes

while I sit
unsaved by my salivation
my unsavory salvation.

Love Is a Fractal

patterns far too complex from any standpoint up close or distanced and yet movement continues happens begins you sit back for the ride to get somepla ce so unexpected and all around you other places a whole world you never sa w before new exciting maybe terrifying ancient not walking being moved being walked constantly moving you cannot eat you cannot sleep you cannot even think a million things you need to do but though you feel you can do an ything you cannot stop it you just keep moving nothing else matters you thin k if you could just pause stand back from a distance take in the whole picture but the whole picture so colossal so unimaginably large no picture conceivabl e in any context rumbled rolling feet never on the ground no sky overhead nothing but constant distraction which you are and you are the attraction co mplete humming concentration asking numbing your chest so you cannot bre athe though all this time you have learned to survive and thrive on nothing bu t the morsels you encounter as you move the past you cannot explain and you have no forewarning of a destination you get a sense others are doing the sam e skating on an ice of unfathomable molecules a bottle full of strong wonder a space with no beginnings and no endings sacrilegious immortality with a ba ckbone of total honesty interconnection with everything more present than pr esent more now than now scratches in the wind no earth no sky only pattern s beautiful patterns so unfettered and spirited you cannot stop please do not let it stop while it lasts its sparkling its spiraling its brevity as unending as the sun

Dune Dream

I wanted to do so much:
tie your arms and legs,
undam my yellow river
on the soft slope of your body
where within your wind-shaped soul
lie ripples, smooth edges, the multitude
of grains perfectly you.
As I trickle down and disappear,
you welcome me into you,
new territory for such a torrent:
       soft and solid, always vacillating.

From those who have explored you before
I find footprints where
I falter in mysterious despair.
Whisper in my ear
tales of these adventures
Promise I am next
       And I will untie you.

Because I want to do so much:
unbury the root bursting with your life
and release my dragon tongue
on this ever-growing tendril,
breathing fire all the while,
waves of blistering heat
through your open
channels up my spine,
with a candle, both ends lit,
leave wax on your trunk
       in the shape of love.

By morning, I am the Sun:
My bright fingers bring your soul to life.
Where your undulous body
meets earth and sky
bleeds a sap from mother's maple
which feeds her desires

        for the sweetness of her flesh.

Toads

You wait long months
spadefoot lodged
in shackles of earth
dry cracked clay slow
motion ponderous
as the world laments
in standstill and people
worry rain
will never come
and all life will end

One day the old sky
grumbles weary of
despair and bitter
roots below
tears escape rising winds
visions burst sorrow
passions pushed beneath
the Earth's body
call the clouds with eyes
looking down for embrace

Then down in clusters
buckets of swollen drops
like plump balloons
holy sky secretions
softening the soil
unfastening your pain
from cemented longing

Clawing your way above
ground in time for white
waters swaggering
a pond you never knew
now home to your love
wet and forgiving
free from stifling confines

Then your ears perk
to seductive songs
like the marimbas
you once fell backwards
and astonished over.

Arroyo

I can see all of you now
teetering on the cut bank
my hand cupped brow
spread fingers braiding sun
that blinds me from you

grateful your most loveliness
swaddled in light
reaches across

         that chasm between us
formed by heavy storms
those seasoned passions
meant to be ours stolen
to open this divide

         We imagine death down there
ending all possibilities
But on the safe edge
of this dry crevasse
grow weary of longing

             looking, wondering, dying alone.

My fluvial veins of healing
forcibly fallow this albatross
a thousand miles from home
caught in a flood of desire
breaching the edge to our loins

which lift us off
joining in the bottoms
meandering their course

flowing to hinterlands risking
starvation beside skeletons
unlucky creatures
prowling predators
springs of desire

we have nothing more to fear
      danger already surrounds us.

Ribbons

The first day of May love comes
beneath beeches and tulip poplars,
naked forest flings fueled with desire

our dearest friends entangled
then caressed by damp dead foliage
fallen the winter before.

Bewitching breezes
rustle those still holding on
and those green ones now leafing out.

Mingling earth and sky brings us this grounded day,
then like a finger in a socket we are struck
by those lost to the other side—

those whose hearts drifted out of range
those still here who might come back
bridging divides, traveling without moving.

The night before, we burned our burdens
out from our within, shouting
them aloud to the flames.

Dropped by exhaustion
we slept and dreamed.
In the morning, amidst the smoke

of piquant incense, the forest beckons.
We answer our sylvan calling, husk its trunk,
in preparation of succession.

But first they say anoint yourself
with morning dew formed fresh
on green ground cover for love

and lust from sunrise to fire-lit night.
In this we unfasten years of fear,
open gates to allow in what fences

of worry kept out. Clothing anointed
with last year's sweat and tears
we tear to strips tied in long lengths

fastened to the arboreal crown.

Then with the unfailing rise of drums
we dance and sing and scream, unleashing
our hearts in every step, breath and howl.

Peels of poplar bark made into bowls
filled with laughing fruits
of reverent colors and profane

flavors served to each other. This love
trapped within comes out
in these glorious

ribbons.

Crazy Bear Mountain

She asks me questions in my sleep.
Will I ever find a home?
Will I stop bursting open my heart
for every companion who walks my path?

She tells me time and again:
Where the grass is greener
hearts beat deeper and earth
swallows spirit into her belly.

And from there erupts a song
tightening loose cords
tying the knot of passions
like crazy old bears.

A song with steep rugged
lyrics like a mountain ditty
with a chorus of green men
sowing beds of refrain

where until death
I will awaken.

Nothing and Everything

I

The mad love fucking
in thunderstorms
The hushed stillness of sky-born tears
tap the roof on our minds above,
drop joy in our hearts below.

II

Touching tendrils deep
in our being
The dark bowels of righteous passion
release the aroma of meaninglessness
from the judgment of "true" love.

III

Heroic hips thrusting
in a new year
Carnal backwaters inter-course forsaken
boundaries drawn across bodies
as waves pummel a breach on our shore.

I Guess We Will Still Have Our Dogs

When we first encountered each other
blazing fall sun across hills sprayed
every shade yellow red green
jelling light to set the stage,
it was our dogs
in their tumbling loving nuzzling
who kindled such envy in me.

Blue skies adept enough to upstage us
if it weren't for our guffawing
together at our bold
companions doting
playing vicarious pleasures
desires un-shamed
few words exchanged.

Shall I return here every day
between these hours
as light settles
in unstoppable winter rest
and we fall back wrenching time?
Where will you be at the first snow
when after lunch the day begins to end?

Though I do not know you
I already miss you. Might our dogs
meet again, and hence you and I?

Getting Somewhere

I never wanted to be something to someone.
But I would be anything to you.
Now, I am nothing.

If only I could see you as anything
less than everything
I might be something to myself.

Everyone wants to find themselves
within theirselves
like the three jewels
in the treasure chest
Bodhisattva goads me to open.

I know this will pass
but I only discern myself in you.
The trove remains concealed.

Breaking

With my love of many years
and another now his love

of not yet as many years,
like the skydiving the year before,

this was really their trip.
This was what he wanted.

His fancy obliged for this season
of the orcas

For they had begun to surface.

From my side of the boat
I could see through the cabin

the two of them side by side
looking out at the water. And yes

the whales were coming but I sensed
another excitement, could almost imagine

them holding hands (were they?)
with anticipation. I chose to turn away

Because who am I to question love?

Just then the captain and crew alerted us
to look off the starboard bow.

There were *oos* and *ahs* as we saw
them just beneath our boat's reflection.

When they emerged through the wake
it was like the elephant in the room

became visible, only this was the pod
breaking, everything large

we had kept at bay.

And I knew with the blur of black on white,
the spouting off of some
needed release deep down,
I would soon be alone.

Love Letters

It must have been
the tail end of the season
in your neck of the woods
when I scratched your back
and you scratched mine and we
passed through our personal belongings
between the openings in our trains of thinking
shooting perilously across the continents of pages,
like walking a knife edge ridge on that mountain
in Maine we both traversed before we met.
Even now in this place of our own without
our pens we walk a narrow path
the depths of the cosmos
and the gods of place
on either side.

One Tennessee Summer

Early in the morning the whippoorwills kept saying
this is life. This is the way life goes. I hadn't slept much.
My bed still empty. My beloved bastion of domestic bliss
out chasing the person he loved
who was chasing the person he loved.
It was summer but the morning cool
and the whippoorwills said stop taking this lying down.

So I went out barefoot to the moonlit garden insects abuzz
walked down rows of pea blossoms smelling that bucolic
    feculence
manure we'd laid down the sweltering day before
and grazed the shoots, early breakfast. All the while
whippoorwill shamans sing this life into being.
The sunlight rising, the roosters arousing spirits of languor

I dreamed my way back to bed, sweet sleep, heartache
    mollified
and again the whippoorwills

this is life this is life this is life.

THE BEAUTY BEFORE US

Read the Warnings and Guidelines Before Proceeding

Love should never come to endless negotiation,
making beautiful arrangements of practicalities
as if they were flowers in an ugly vase;

or discussing the practicality of arrangements
like love was approaching the end of its life
and we needed to choose its casket.

Love should never end in a brewing swill of sorrow
drowning the history of joy with its contents
as if the melancholy had no end;

or spewing the histories at the ground
like their elixirs were suddenly so bitter
a single sip would poison.

Bachelor

Five boneless fish sticks, two pieces barbecued tofu,

and a sliced zucchini in a 1-minute marinade
air fried in my instant pot and washed down
with double bitter ale called "Sip of Sunshine."

Simple joy.

I always find the first bite loneliness
this time of evening when we would regale
each other with stories and anecdotes

struck silent by dare we say the absence of love?

When I leave the house I feel compelled to share
my plans with someone who might care if I never
return, but she quips she is not my mother

in a way that cuts my invincible core.

Shall I grab another to heal the wound?
I'll smoke on it and then decide my time
is best spent writing down the bones

missed as I picked through dinner.

Museum

Somewhere in this house lies a lost curio
like an ancient coin made of priceless joy
they never knew they had.

The curators say such was their love,
stamped in affirmations of lives worth sharing,
then rolled across the floor, forgotten under a rug.

Love no longer in currency loses
its value behind the glass display,
a relic of what was once purely theirs.

Beginnings of the End

Maybe it was the first time I raged at the machine
my patience with technology at its end
the time I answered your proposal
with aren't we already married?
When I said my initial attraction
was not erotic and insisted
you fast with me every year
so I could find my way
Perhaps it was then

when what could have been a new beginning
sent me off making end of life plans
maybe I'll die here, maybe there
what does it matter when love
is bound for plummeting
the steep edge in view

So I climb
to mountaintops
and feel the woven detritus
beneath my driving feet on the mother
who gives birth to everything I embrace
time for diversion and distraction
withstand the riotous river rapids
know perils reward the living
and that decisive sundown
will finally come.

Spring Equinox

I mother this vicissitude
like my only child
born twice a year.

On the lighter side of darkness,
the edge of these emaciated woods,
I wonder if the opening will ever come.

Then, walking through the forest,
I come upon an infant Arcas
and the fruits he offers –

    Cherry blossoms wafting
    Rubensian scents, zaftig
    green foliating rays of sun

I hold this herbaceous babe
enwrapped in my lap.
We will feed upon each other.

Remembering Last Year at Hood Canal

This time last year we were paddling together
in deep roiling waters in Hood Canal.
Checking crab traps for that catch
to feed the joyful celebration of our mother.

For she had become my mother, too.

We paddled well the two of us: a left, then a right.
If too much on the left a stroke or two on the right.
This was how we went through life:
On course for a future I thought I knew

to a point farther away than it first had appeared.

That night we had crab and laughed and drank together.
Then we stood in the dark in the ocean breeze.
The sailor in my blood knew we'd been blown off course.
Our love irrevocably lost overboard

sent to the bottom along with the weight of empty words.

Sometimes I stand on this different shore
See him on the boat fading into beyond
Everyday a little farther
Less and less I know him.

And less and less I remember.

The Beauty Before Us

We must fall in love with beastly things
Lascivious brash and pithy things
Bend our knee in grace of circumstance
Braid misgivings in tales of radiance
Forgiveness received, offenses softened
Surrender to expanding beauty
Engendering bonds, give birth, belonging
Falling down before our calling
Falling down before our calling
To see the beauty in all the living,
Resting, breathing, brave in grieving.

Ruminations on a Phone Call from an Old Crush

I thought when you called
after all those years
you were going to tell me
you loved me

That after all those years
you had come to feel
you loved me
you just couldn't say

You had come to feel
I was so indelibly in you
you just couldn't say
you were in love with me

I was so indelibly in you
I was done prowling for love
because you were in love
love had returned to me

I was so done prowling for love
a loathsome waste of time
I thought love had returned to me
Your moment married to someone else

a loathsome waste of time
so you were coming back for me
though married to someone else
and then I thought how thoughtless

to think you were coming back for me
to stop my longing for your love
I thought how thoughtless of me
with your wife still by your side

not to stop my longing for your love
your daughters now grown
your wife still by your side
This is what I thought when you called.

Rebuilding from Wonder

Digging up dreams again.
Piling up the agonies into ecstasy
of the end that's about starting over.

Then upon waking:
The dread of impossibility
unearths itself.

So I must fill this chasm
with shovel by shovel of wonders
to hold me from despair

smooth the gravel
of unsettled regrets
and tamp out the stale air.

From this level ground
I can build again.

Beloved

Yesterday my sleep opened up to the stars
              and in my dream a stampede
"Where is my beloved?" I cried
to an ever-widening void
for something,
anything draped in love
even the unknown,
to rein in again
what we cannot live without.

That is love:
What we cannot anything without,
which without freezes us dreamless
uninspired to move. Today

love rides a horse of endless possibility
              into a certain mysterious future.
Without love, a beast of misery,
rotted grief   faded familiarity
caking hooves   splattering knees,
With love rein-free he races
in wild resolve
unbridled untamed
embraces unknowns.

This is love:
What carries us beyond the saddling,
that which bears illumination
bucks up imagination.

Cowboy Regrets

Some people get thrown from their horse
and get right back on.
If I take the time to get to know a horse
gently mounting its back
engaging in giving and receiving
and it throws me to the ground
horse riding may not be my thing.

What would it take to get up after a fall
unlike so many greenhorns before
and take the reins again?
To find love in what I'm doing
and do what I love?
Whatever it is.
To know the wounds
from that unintended dismounting
would heal in their own time.
To desire something
Anything.
To go somewhere
even a distant place.
To get back on and feel the wind
blow the journey over me.
To not know what I will find.
Expect nothing.
Revel in everything.

The Things I Can Now See Without You

I saw an indigo bunting today
and thought of you.
Of how I know birds make you happy
and how I wished happiness came as easily to me.
How life thrives when we see things
we usually fail to see
Like impossibly blue birds
Or those heart gems: the people
I would be lesser for not having known.
That my shirt was on inside out
My collar folded in
Or the delightful strangeness of euphorbia
Eagles perched on highway posts
Flowers growing out of rocks.
Yes, today I saw this bird
and I had to let you know
I'm learning to notice things
though I no longer share it all with you.

How to Start Over

Sometimes the lights
go out. The stars you were following
now immersed in hopeless darkness.

When love died at the hands
of some formidable presence
I dug in my heels and wailed to no avail.

As those memories implode
in the fallows of now I see
good fortune poisoned by pains of the past.

From the ends of everything,
when they truly come, can the good
plant seeds of something new?

To have loved
may indeed be a seed for a life worth living.
But such platitudes do not instruct

how to let go
how to start over
with not a spark of imagination.

It has been said
the depth of love is
measured by the magnitude of grief.

I have loved deeply
then this life. For the earth moved
beneath when the winds bore the clouds

and that star I watched
closely faded to dark bringing
not the end but new uprisings, a revolution.

My heart ruptures its defenses
opening a crack in the sidewalk and there
along the gray boulevard of despair bursts the purple iris.

ABOUT THE POET

Growing up around hills and lakes in New Jersey, northwest of New York City, Buffy Aakaash has moved between small towns, big cities, and rural queer communities for the last almost forty years, farming, writing, growing food, and doing healing work. Engaged in poetry most of his life, he is inspired by the beings both human and non-human in the many places he has lived, visited, and explored—New Mexico high deserts, several big cities, the US west coast, Tennessee's hills and hollers, as well as extensive travels in Mexico. Currently, he resides in Vermont's Green Mountains with his four-legged fellow traveler/hiker, Bodhi the pug.

Aakaash's poems have been published by *Sweety Cat Press, New Feathers, Main Street Rag, The Brussels Review,* and numerous others. He authored the 2022 chapbook, *Untangling the Knots,* which was nominated for the Vermont Book Awards. His poem "The Beauty Before Us" won the Poetry Society of Vermont's 2022 Marion Gleason Memorial Award. In 1994 Aakaash received an MFA in playwriting from Columbia University. In addition to being a writer, he freelances as a media designer and manuscript editor. Some of his previously published poetry can be viewed at www.BuffyAakaashPoetry.com.